Burnt Mountain

Kuhl House Poets

Lisa Wells and Joshua Marie Wilkinson, series editors

Mark Levine, advisory editor

Burnt Mountain

Emily Wilson

University of Iowa Press ❧ Iowa City

University of Iowa Press, Iowa City 52242

uipress.uiowa.edu
Printed in the United States of America
Printed on acid-free paper
Design by Sara T. Sauers

Name: Wilson, Emily, 1968– , author.
Title: Burnt Mountain / by Emily Wilson.
Description: Iowa City: University of Iowa Press, 2025. |
Series: Kuhl House Poets
Identifiers: LCCN 2025004994 (print) |
LCCN 2025004995 (ebook) |
ISBN 9781685970307 (paperback; acid-free paper) |
ISBN 9781685970314 (ebook)
Subjects: LCGFT: Poetry.
Classification: LCC PS3623.I58 B87 2025 (print) |
LCC PS3623.I58 (ebook) |
DDC 811/.6—dc23/eng/20250522
LC record available at https://lccn.loc.gov/2025004994
LC ebook record available at https://lccn.loc.gov/2025004995

To Nickey & Don Wilson

Contents

Burnt Mountain

Fernery

The ferns are rising off their fern-stitched stems
bowling outward sprigged spirals
into those turns in the river's
tumbled ramps and slot slopes
the ferns are rising
along the river through its glades
in styptic ostrich-feather flows and royal feints
the lobular sensitives the common cinnamon
fiery ferns checking
from their stems
among the grids
of loose and inter-hemming roots
the headiest trend
against all rivers
mingling redoubling
that vintage ferny hurl across the corridor
toward dark-empaneled woods
none can shut them

Heath Obscure

so close to it the trail trails
into it the sumptuary

crumble underfoot the meanly
spangled mollusk grays

the bumps and slides I had to
sense against its harsh

thickets up and down the
stuckness ardent incomplete the

cushion sinks the ground-
expounding roots

scrub up through it

The Pink

I have to go out there to see
what's pink in the tall wet grass

standing there next to the yellow
mullein spike, the soluble yellow

pink and something I can't place
in the cosmos, flourishing topmost

filleting a groove
in the brain, caught

waiting to be let outside
wanting to know

what roosts in the tall webbed glaucousness
a flame-out or a picture

a cloven or a pink
pretext before mass consuming sunlight.

Deplorables

Who wields itself in the bog's ruin?
The arrowhead.

Who spikes the low-watt red-wired roadside scrub?
The spreading dogbane.

Whose cramped leaf folds the dark under its deck?
The giant burdock.

Who stalls the grass wherein we lurk?
The black-eyed susan. The campion.

Who did this to us?
The cranesbill.

Who did this to us?
The hoary mint. The false solomon.

The Wood

Someone's always cutting something somewhere
the saw blade says
deep in the wood
the wood revolves, returns
perfect spruce buds flecked from
the stalk

across the spongy ground
fuzzed in the formal
succulent mire-black boot-work
someone's done

the cutting, zeroing
spicular off
the moon-green-gauzy functionaries—
drag them, ditch them, feed them
into the batch the trees stand
up, woodsmen

deep in the col, somewhere
always boring
some way through
the whorled tooth

The Rain

Will I find there nothing
nothing rakes the summer woods
no light, no rain, no rain spell mustering
the packed leaves, sods
of softened leaves, the same

Nothing shouldn't speak
of nothing where, nothing of
the cropped exchange, verdant usage, love
nothing hardly stooped
the ferning grain

Nothing is so nothing nearly
ceded, graduating scaffold
scaping off our tree
who says you won't grow cold
the rucking fail-safes

Nothing, in the field, no
nothing, the briefness of that
turning under the plain
far-off thunder, begs on
the smell of the rain

The Boulder

deep in its visages
implications crossing back

and down streaking the sides
where it cracked apart

the shoulder boulders tumbled in a pile
threads spun clothing them

hurled suspended
all the fretfuls lost begun

mossed forgotten ton
the wind the rain

whose wild drops flame
the blistered cups

Attention

a small thing produced
red blips at the tops

of its stalks standing
where a forest mulched

the butte of a stripped
stump—

flaring beaded palest
green dotted curled and

cracked along the studs
the silver's rotting

tinted turkey-tails off
the bark if you paid

Erratica

A form like a fern cladding soft adages against

A carpet moss under which the boulder tangents off

Old subtle cop-outs all in pile-up

Stenciled horns pegged pyrola bells inky probes and

Global umbel

From the split furl coming

Across it here on the ground it

Floats the grosser woods-work done it

Forks again

Cirque

Off a summer edge
in brusque spruce maneuvering
over the stones, into rifts
and slots of cobble-stacked
up-endedness
exposed in stipple scrub
the die-cut spiky lichen-
crush and ash, in spent
laurels, the wildly weirdly
low-bush sprawling habits of—
crowberry, partridgeberry—all
the fledge-laced Labrador tea
slanting its load
weatherward over-
tilting broken through
the round that was made, once
staking where it
strips and shreds
outlaid strange
sought vantages

Roundleaf

Spare, sparred and
tender green, porcelain-
    green collocations

shot from the darker stem
stifled around afloat
    the hasped household

orbiting in this
sump accrued among
    boulders, canting

masked with moss
hung inside the
    pitching shades

redundances—
fleshy abstract
    rapt

root striking—
lofted, alone—
    off a mountain!

Redoubt

One keeps oneself apart
from the brute world
keeps oneself off

In woods yes
alters the cloud puts
pocks on the mountain

Gleams then wipes
out gleams
marking that place

One keeps for oneself
the girding
glypting spruces' terrain

Turns and begins to
break down this
brittlest scene skirted

Bits of its cones

Loose Triad

I can't think about you all the time

The trail smears, fusc-

Russet, ferns in a crux, rouge stem-hairs, surly involucres

The dead crowd and flout their green survivals—here

Here you are—from a dark mud, from a burned-out excess

Waxed shafts forking into triangles

Knitted with care, the care, the lavishes, the slants, the one-off

Beastly embroideries

Up through the woods, forcing the stones

Shelving mushrooms cleave

The fretted chuck

All antithesis leaning inward, rock on rock on

Fir growing out the tunnel crack

Bricked from the base

Just pieces of it, wildering around it, chipped cones

The cortices, papery seed-shingle

Something catches in the mouth that

Crushes it

Crows beset the settled hawk

In balm poplars, brittling the bastes

Get away from me fuck off

You fucking fuckers

Crows stoking up that slacker hawk

High in its handiwork

All the crows crying for their plot

The distant scene-stealing tourist plane

Twirling the mountain top

Cousin ravens reaving those

Steeps off it

Ragged Robin

Ragged ruddy run
your pink mess
right up my path

your splinted
spittle-spunking bulb
your rubbed

doublet triple-knit and
vacuum slit
I must not like you

rugged rose
slacked in your jam
come off it

done-up undone
wit as wit
cracks me a care

into this shrill
rufous thought you
steel infringer

Animus

A marked man
in your proud
stance at the edge
of my wood

A markèd specimen
shagged with oakmoss
lowermost slats
bole craped

The color of brass polish
have I loved
even as you cast
midway along rotaries

Of plaint and chastening
I drift all day
your trademark shade
would not but

This starked up
expressly for

truce or displace

Happy Comical Crewelwork Panel

Birds are masters of men
and rodents a-roll on this bluish
citrine lithos sprung
with vines delicate bells
bothering the Dutchman's pipe
forcing off the simple
stems midstream mid-pageant-
ing beneath the scoriaceous
corded pines the buff
slinks the worked trunk
stagnant golden pears of
very giants careful
under that
branch don't come
down on your little slug
brain crowded with
but you are a man
the scaled tuberose
plows into us

Interrupted Fern

Fronds begetting fronds aligning spurning

The rakes the seams parting the spore the

Spore the tissuey fuming with this with this that

Parts the putting off a radiance

Splits the mid-stalk dwindling the thickening

Stop

At the twist-off

Sterile perfoliate hours come up

The neoprene bluebead lilies come

Up bell down if you like that's a foot

Soldier ground-sucking Day-Glo slime on a

Touched it over it

Dead Color

Gradate the mud!
Subdue the dust!
Extract from jarring darks
the objects faulted
patched and slurred
in Vandyke brown or
Hooker's green
in separate layings on
or under burls
of your watchfulness.
The pestilence of gray
and lilac gray
you must point toward
the furnaces!
Nature being vile
more ways than one.
This touch for the ghastly!
This total ignorance of
tree structure!

Potentilla

Pale sulfur discus flicker
trying to catch some one again
sun gets you staring not
for any other.

What's so mesmerizing to the one
who snags you, showy berry
runner up a shadow side, hide
where you've gone.

The silver-damask skies
the razor-purled ways
look out for one another
says the rose.

Outside Art

What can be done with this plastic
fantabulous part

the river squigs through
its multiple woodlot

hung just rained in
so few wordings

crank the round
"vetch" "brake" "everlastings" "and"

stock-sided grasses swung
how long this slow

gravure on
the mind to be plain

Yard Work

Riddled brown the birches
Gullying through the somewhat seen
Root up the raspberries, axe the ashes
Overly complicate slashing down-yard

Whether to leave them local mades
Of great bleaching grounds
Run into sometimes
Out in the woods' barricades . . .

A bridal clematis rigors up alders
Haws, hollies, colonizers
Daisy and hay-scented fern, crimp-clover
Parasol-tops, goldenrods, moneywort, succory

Cutting the clearing/place-staking cruelly
Frees fierce topiaries

Verbascum

Taller than a man
pitched from the earth
garbled needle
tracking now
its volute screed
bee- and beetle-ridden
up and down between
the un-
sprung buds, the wild
efficient feel of
smocked
rabbit-skinned
explosions
poised so slowly
on its undertaking—
the cold and the craftless—
was not craft
spotting the niches
the leaves the
xanthene core

Let Beauty Be

painstakingly
across fallen rocks
wound aground on
the vigilant rocks
tenebrous outcrops
opening or clamped
rooty or bruised
the “gum periwinkle cucumber dulse”
ensnarling
some not some nor
piercing stranger
upright rage
primed over
known or unknown
tweaked and tried in
tedium
fixed with fixed points

Hoop

No more than this.
Rhythm flocking its parts.

Clangors felted into.
The blanket heave.

Trucks coasting the road.
Pinpricks. Chickadees.

Thinner harsher bands of.
I don’t want.

Don’t I want.
Such grades in the lace.

Edged lady ferns.
Stripping into you.

The Puck

What was it in the woods that made me see
The path I couldn't make though in a dream
I webbed its slits together as I saw
Them coming through, pashed twigs and branches
Whatever I saw and couldn't see converging
Trundling the burrowed brook stones
A rain that visited, flooded and vamped
Prodded and prunted up dead drift
In little channels, dark down a hillside
Those bevelments cut starlike, so, black
Trails of stars kinked out in darkness
What woods became of a coursing dream
One stood at the door, that far-forged interior
Outlandish green and flaming cause unknown

Convolvulus

granulating grays
branches grasses

tinkerings of
the signature

thing the tree is
pitting against

curly dendroid
crusts occasional lichen

yellow plasms and
the tactical

white wormy
buds gearing up from the twigs the

nothing
ness they were

enameled from

Sampler

Several stitches, several catches, mounting stinted greens

Churls of green, forks, flaunts around a trunk

The rip-stop snarled bladder sedge, the bluebead's trilobe jigged

About its stalk, some perforated dogwood bracts

Milky pink with minute bristle-scutes the woodfern scrawls

And clashes—depths

Depths come compoundingly

Never end, do and

Where what heaven was was

Plain & Fancy

Functional in gloom
the lupine rods bent out
from the gravel

Firs that drift
around just
once catch in the craws—

Fust-purple glowering green
helleborine
fix yourself up

Your miracle
mishapped in the yard
the what was even worried over

Hacked about it
burdocking, burgling
a way up

Out of it
being
a tough invasive bitch

Okay

Esker

Deep in the woods, in the bent of the brook,
with its polypody flicks and its clear
air of density, dense mystery
and grayness striating tall as a sound
small house, this boulder of an aged
overworked interest, in the interest of
scapular rigid black and frosted lichens
all wreckage at the base, a rooted thing
uprooted, slovenly imposed, not rooted.

Summer River

The river's never done.
It keeps things clear
around the broad mound
of river stones the winter
put behind, the winter
river trussed with ice
it mottled in and under
over stones it pushed
and bunted, tampered up
to stump-corrals, into
boulder bins, the carved
woeful ancient straits
à la mode, or moded-
out, the winter spent
the summer shunted self
can never remember
seasons over seasons borne of stones
rounded, rackled into charmed
rotted broken eddy
grounds, and the fern stowages
dank graded harbors
under alders where
the bedstraw burns and crowns.

Poplars

Sun in poplar leaves
bronze and green, green-and-
umber-whirled brief
arrangements
pinned and pulled
wads of wind the sun
can only influence, friend
the times being what
not even poplars under
stand, the sun the wind
through ragged-ravaged
leaves, the flagrant service
wanted in us.

The Grade

Weedy forgotten places along the grade
To stand, in the open, suddenly
A mountain steering down its dark
Out of rank woods buffeted
Weedy fragrant fraught on the grade
Thready buds of hawkweed
Sway the sallow clover under bezeled-
Rosy meadowsweet hovering the sedge
A sacristy of weeds in weed-chock
Broken beds of silvered slash
Trash of a forest pitched
Wherever you turn turn the glamour
River turnings of that grade
Itself the iron-jolted bracken

Zoochorous

Frisking movements
outward, into the blush
late boneset, mist flower

plunging open forked, flopped, blow-notes
in stunning reversals
haven't we seen this one before

unlike any other
with rocket goosefoot pearly everlasting mugwort stumps
on the far side

watching something shock the margins
where it clung, everlastings
never get anywhere with you

Hourglass Pond

Breaking inward into
the cloud cavity, vitreous
swirls rust and fern
cut mask cameo cedar clamp

Poke-pins of the dead
sparring horizontally
one against each other
what do I know

Amn't even in the picture
anymore dropped out
scuffing the nobody
stones bulked at the edge

Cramming clouds and
spatterdock just
get clear of this

Interim

What if the spirit in these times
kept going
up the long shoulder
spruce brush/scrub on either
side crating the dark
slabs cornering
drainages glistering
the rock
onyx and parded
kept on being
no where to be seen but
spiked
all over
the place whatever
it was
tendrilled caterpillar
spoolwork
crossing the leaf
it all broke down in
who said
not backing to the
trees moved on to the next

Notch

One is apt to strategize
—wedges and blocks,
back-knits, flinching up
the wall along the cracks

Traveling texturally, into
the boulder jumble, where
to clamp on is ditching half
your filaments, down a

Sheer interface, subway, hinter-
place, flocked mysterious
gels packed dubiously—
rolled up edgewise—

Glisten, if you come
the way through

Little Estival

Summer ranges up
the summer mountain
Osmund's ferns spout
their glossy flanges

August takes its time
developing stilt rocks
the pungent flux of
the interium

Spots between the blank
gashes in the paper
birches utter
ly fresh peeled pink

Grassy Loop

Isn't it the burden
to break things down

The wave of wind at summer's end
along a field or wood

Retracting in and out of cloud
shadow, the gust-run

Incremented hours pass
through the blades, the wood begins

The bulrush towers
ceding purple embers on that ground

And return to
the taut instrument

Pastiche

Something in the graces getting us
up through the trees

drifting zones befalling thus—
striped maples, paper birch

hobblebushes sprung with flies
the tensed hemlock, the outride larch

the true fir and the spruce
the dwarf willow, the willow-

worsted heath angled low
over the stones—

the laurels' spice
shooting through the stones—

the laurels grounding thus
the stones

Twistedstalk

Along the ledges
the ribbed rock
root-work twining

up more or less
with a wren's sound's
spates and verges

the way it comes
over-woven
to be cleared

split from the trail's
crop-offs—
things tugged and

wounded with their blades
flails and fervencies
that show now

under the rickrack
perfect leaves
the berries blaze

Going Up

the windy side, blue
tints the summer mountains northward
or heavenward
if there is no heaven
but clouds crowding off their tagged
surfaces, that spirit brunting
mountains into clouds
impressionless astounding
stark-streamed
before we reach it

Burnt Mountain

The hoist upward into that land
loaded at the top—

wild raisin, mountain
ash, the alder and the stout

fir and the glaring hair moss—oh
this instant—reached—again

again the open summit cracks
and fire brazes the gray

rocks under fire-coal lichens,
dark gyrons into

the white-throat's strike off
point of a spruce

Nine Block (Autumn)

All the woods in orange now
beech and maple shaking off
the worked wirings

Branches and trunks blotched and marked
acid white, the dozing
glosses drift them

Impressing themselves, suddenly
yellow oxides shot with green
hand axes drop

Sulfurous maples and firs and pines
standing around where
the raspberries, reddish, curl

Now the sky foists into
that crazy red sumac
"soldier color"
a wave through the beeches
burnishing—
what the slacks are doing within
such rightness—
Terrorizing. Terror with furor, mixed
tipped toward blear.
Gears and chainworks and the
calibrated field of plant pigments
the sky is powering into
tapering the quick plates
strapped golds, a last maple
there in the woods
rutilating—

Which parts are they part of
stubbed from the rocks.
Sedges. Mosses. Winter
lichens stitched with black,
crimson trefoil rosids
working hard to man the frank
surfaces, rocks, ruins of rocks
busted and cut, the sinking slow
bulwark of Burnt Mountain.
Which parts are beneath.
Failed state, bloodied enterprise.
Rocks in the river
of rock the mountain was.
Parts unneeded, parts
needed to be necessary,
here, the fractal greens
against their boulders rage.

How to keep going, going on
as the firs keep forking
their minted cones, massive
grillworks, and the mosses
their gilded flicks, their slender
cups that writhe in the sun
and the soot disks of the toadskin
and the acrylics of the baneberries.
How to keep going, forward, on, into
the feverish track toward
beginning to offer it, to make it
hold, your end up in
this stereo constellation
synthetic haven
blunted with frost
likenesses like

Nothing to be done.
The sun made the flies come out
and they are sacking the windows,
heroically. I would spare them.
The long toil to the steep drop-off.
Flaming around around,
little asteroids.
It's too warm in here,
October, supposedly,
the leaves fallen, almost all,
on the trail, scuffing yellowish
pink where the beeches
dominate. I am to "savor" them,
the woods, I can see
where I walked, the ridge line
crossing the foam-bright
slides, lichens bunching thick and
whitewash green, greenish grays
advanced in the grades of stiffening,
smack-red vacciniums
clumped and the leathery gills
and the grooved black getaways.

What's live what's dying
out in the woods
the season stakes its stead
What litters amber
leaves along
the path leans unmade

North wind
took it over
to hook on a gusset pine
Who fritters now the
sun the chill
blazons in

Winding that road, shouldering
its still-work, rocks, rockiness
several ditch drawn ravages
asters, goldenrod, pits where it
climbs, where passages break out
slumps, ground-ruts, washed-
out fringes, loose rock that was
some trail or brook bed, both
rugged, contingent.
Over the road it rigs our mind
into it, turning, touching
the rock points—
the mountain around us.

"I know I am saying too much
not letting things go
slipping things under mucking too close
you don't want me telling you what to do"

"Coming off the summit yesterday
two chickadees gnarled in conversation—
'Hi, hi there'—very vexedly
what this must look like to you"

"All those times I sang so you could sleep
have you forgotten them
the ferns around here
still 'go'-light green"

Spikes and cleavers
mud, black mud
in delves between

the stones, dead is
don't you know

sometimes barely
going but what is
can't be but you

think it should

be ablaze under
rocks and stones
the glutty rush the
smote lobelia and
                in its slot
brimming hinged not

moving outright

Acknowledgments

MANY THANKS to the editors of the following journals for publishing these poems in earlier versions: *Ploughshares* ("Verbascum"); *Chicago Review* ("The Rain," "Roundleaf," "Redoubt," "Hourglass Pond," "Notch," "Twistedstalk"); *Lana Turner* ("Deplorables," "Erratica," "Plain & Fancy"); *can we have our ball back?* ("The Wood," "Happy Comical Crewelwork Panel," "Interrupted Fern," "Dead Color," "Convolulus," "Interim"); *Annulet* ("Loose Triad," "Outside Art," "Sampler," "The Grade," "Burnt Mountain").

My thanks also to Josh Wilkinson and Lisa Wells, and to Jim McCoy, Meghan Anderson, and everyone at the University of Iowa Press. I am indebted to Sara T. Sauers for the design of this book.

Thank you, Everett and Gideon Levine, for your willingness and enthusiasm for the hike. Thank you, Mark Levine, for faith, everything.

Kuhl House Poets

CHRISTOPHER BOLIN
Anthem Speed
Ascension Theory
Form from Form

SHANE BOOK
All Black Everything
Congotronic

ONI BUCHANAN
Must a Violence
Time Being

MICHELE GLAZER
fretwork
On Tact, & the Made Up World

DAVID MICAH GREENBERG
Planned Solstice

JEFF GRIFFIN
Lost and

HAJAR HUSSAINI
Disbound

JOHN ISLES
Ark
Inverse Sky

YOUNA KWAK
For This and Other Cruelties

JESSICA LASER
The Goner School

AARON MCCOLLOUGH
Rank
Salms

RANDALL POTTS
Trickster

BIN RAMKE
Airs, Waters, Places
Matter

MICHELLE ROBINSON
The Life of a Hunter

VANESSA ROVETO
bodys
a women

ROBYN SCHIFF
Revolver
Worth

SARAH V. SCHWEIG
Take Nothing with You

ROD SMITH
Deed

DONNA STONECIPHER
Transaction Histories

COLE SWENSEN
The Book of a Hundred Hands
Such Rich Hour